FIREFIGHTER'S

"Little Black Book"

Your Pocket Guide To Safety

Stan Tarnowski
Fire Chief (Ret.)

www.5AlarmMedia.com

Cover artwork by Randall Oelze

Foreword and editing by Chief Robert Avsec (Ret)

ISBN: 978-1-387-50414-5

PublishNation LLC
www.publishnation.net

Table of Contents

18. When driving the Chief's car

19. Driving apparatus – emergency and non-emergency

20. Taking apparatus to the supermarket, Home Depot, etc.

21. Personal hygiene and overall cleanliness

22. Work and dress uniforms

23. Use of alcohol and/or drugs on or off duty

24. Gambling at the Fire Station on or off duty

25. Pornography at the Fire Station

26. Video cam usage at the Fire Station on and off duty

27. Smart phone use for texting/sexting

28. Picture taking at the Fire Station

29. Outside visitors at the Fire Station

30. Family members at the Fire House

31. Watching TV/movies at the Fire Station

32. Personal space between each other

33. Inappropriate touching between members

34. Sexually explicit magazines of any kind

35. Male and female firefighter qualification and performance

36. Showing respect for each other

37. Starting rumors about a co-worker

38. Picture taking at the scene and sharing

39. Acting professional in all jobs

40. How you personally act on and off duty

41. Family cluster at the Fire Station

42. Profanity at the Fire Station

FOREWORD

I am happy to write this foreword for Chief (Ret.) Stan Tarnowski's second eBook: *Firefighters' "Little Black Book" – Your Pocket Guide to Safety – Top 50 Do's and Don'ts for Today's Firefighter.* Chief Tarnowski provides a modern day, to the point, guide of Dos and Don'ts for all fire service personnel, from the newest rookie to the fire chief.

In today's fire service there are many hurdles and stumbling blocks that any of us can fall over which can destroy a reputation or career or family. How? By not conducting ourselves as professionals at all times and not adhering to a high standard of ethics, morals, respect, and honor for all members of our personal and fire department families.

We are reminded of such "career ending events" through daily news reports of incidents involving financial malfeasance, illegal drug use, illicit sex and Internet pornography, and sexual harassment, just to name a few, that occur in both the public and private sectors. Increasingly, we see this type of poor decision-making taking place by individuals in the fire service as illustrated by some "ripped from the headlines" events:

- "City settles $1.2-million-dollar sexual harassment case against Fire Chief"
- "Four City Firefighters Terminated Over Running Prostitution Ring Out of Firehouse"
- "Paramedic Fired for Posting Accident Photos on Social Media"
- "Fire Department Treasurer Found Guilty of Embezzling $450K from Department Accounts"

We in the fire service must realize just how vulnerable we all are to making similar terrible career ending choices by doing things we know are wrong.

Chief Tarnowski offers a simple and practical guide with this book to help us all keep it on the "straight and narrow" in these challenging times. As trusted public servants (ours is one of the most respected professions in the USA according to most polls on the subject) we all have a duty and responsibility to uphold that trust and integrity that our families and fellow citizens expect from us. Chief Tarnowski's book is sure to become as standard a piece of firefighter equipment as our helmet.

Battalion Chief (Ret.) Robert Avsec
Chesterfield County (VA) Fire and EMS Department

ACKNOWLEDGEMENTS

To: My family
For their love and support and for inspiring me every day.

To: Chief Robert Avsec (Ret)
For his friendship and professional guidance

To: Chief Dennis Rubin (Ret)
For his friendship and mentoring throughout the years

INTRODUCTION

After serving three decades as a firefighter who progressed through the ranks to become a fire chief, I thought this may be the time to share my thoughts on how all firefighters and officers can better serve. Not necessarily from a physical command perspective, but from a personal character perspective. I call it "leading from the front"—regardless of your rank—through daily conduct that is morally and ethically sound.

I wish I could tell you that I have always acted that exact way, and followed my religious beliefs. But I cannot. I, myself have experienced a fall from grace. I wrote these words in 2015 as an inmate in a federal correctional facility where I had served a four-year sentence because of my elicit pornography activities on a popular social media site that was being monitored by federal law enforcement agents searching for elicit pornography activity through a 'Sting' operation. 'Remember ALL Words Matter'.

Through the grace of my Creator and the unyielding support of my family and friends, I'm slowly working to rebuilding a life that I brought down with a series of poor choices. But trust me, it's not easy and I hope nobody has to endure a similar experience. That's why I've written this book.

In my 30 years of serving in the Fire and Emergency services, I have had an opportunity to be around and work with all types of people. They have been people of different races, ethnicities, genders, cultures, religions, and sexual orientations. People from the waterfront of Boston, Ma., throughout Europe, the Middle East, and North America, there is one thing I've learned, and that is that no matter where firefighters are located, the issues are always the same.

They say "people will be people", and I can personally attest to that. I've been fortunate to meet and work with all types of personalities (mostly Type A), those with personal quirks and those with staunch beliefs about everything from sports to cars, trucks, race, religion, politics and much more. Firefighters are no different as they have their preference in firefighting tools and equipment, apparatus manufacturing and their most favored and non-favored co-workers.

If I said firefighters are opinionated, I would be making the biggest understatement of the century! Having said all of that, the *Firefighters' Little Black Book: Your Pocket Guide to Safety* is another tool in the tool box, that if used daily, will help you to become the "best" man or woman you can be in the eyes of your family, friends, co-workers, church friends and the community you serve.

Being a public safety servant as a firefighter in any community is, and should be considered a blessing, and that responsibility should be of great importance to you at all times.

Having said that, this book's subtitle, *Your Pocket Guide to Safety*, refers to the safety of your integrity, ethics, morals and overall ability to make sound, mature and responsible decisions in everything you do, both on the job and off.

This means *everything* you do, both on and off duty. We must never forget that we, as community firefighters have been automatically entrusted by the public we serve. This also means that the public has a natural tendency to trust us with their lives, and all that is precious to them at any given moment where we have been called to assist in some way.

They trust that with every interaction with one of their family members we will perform in an ethically and morally sound manner and have their true interest at heart. Hearing that alone gives me the chills. Twenty-four/seven a total stranger will open their homes to us and allow us inside to help fix their problems, knowing they can trust us. We are "their firefighters."

What is integrity? Integrity can be summed up as "keeping a promise." When we become firefighters the public places their trust in us: trust that we know how to do our job, that we will always do our job to the best of our ability and that we will do our job with impartiality. When we fail to uphold any one of those promises, we break that sacred trust that the public has entrusted to us. And once that trust is broken, it can be very difficult—if not impossible—to regain.

Your *Pocket Guide to Safety Top 50 Do's and Don'ts for Today's Firefighters* is a simple tool that should be used as a daily reminder of how much a difference we make to those we serve and to our family members. None of them ever want to see us fall from grace. This is why I have taken this time to write these simple steps that can change your life.

"A *costume* is something you put on and pretend that you are what you are wearing. A *uniform* on the other hand, reminds you that you are, in fact what you are wearing."—Eunice McGarrahan.

This message reminds me of the first day of firefighter training. We all took off our civilian clothes and put on our uniforms. Each day after that the uniform we put on reminded us that we had entered a period of disciplined training designed to change our attitudes and actions.

Which are you now wearing? A *costume* or a *uniform?*

#1. Be Kind

Webster's Dictionary says this about the word "kind":
"Being kind is an essential character found in a person. It encompasses being sympathetic, gentle, benevolent, understanding, gracious, agreeable and pleasant."

I am sure that you can remember times when you were not kind, or gracious to a family member or friend. Perhaps you were unsympathetic to a patient, disagreeable to your wife or husband, or unpleasant to your mother, father, children, siblings, or co-workers.

We all can do a better job with this very essential human characteristic, especially as firefighters where the root of our existence depends upon our ability to show kindness and compassion in the face of tragedy. Wouldn't it be great to have a "Pre-Daily Checklist" to help you get every day off to a great start? Well here it is!

Daily Check List:
* ❖ Am I – Patient?
* ❖ Am I – Sympathetic to the needs of others?
* ❖ Am I – Gentle and Benevolent, especially for those who can do nothing for me?
* ❖ Am I – Patient and Understanding?
* ❖ Am I – Gracious and Agreeable?
* ❖ Am I – Pleasant to be around?
* ❖ Am I – Morally Sound?

I'm confident that if you review this short list before you start your day, and do those things, you will be amazed how much better you will feel. And I'm sure that those people around you will feel it as well! Trust me, I've been on both sides, and being on the positive side is a better way to live.

#2. Station Duties

No job is too big or too small.

I remember my first station cleaning detail when I was with the Logan Airport Fire Department in 1975. I had just been appointed to the job and here I was being assigned to clean the men's locker room, which included (obviously) the toilets and urinals. (No separate women's locker room yet).

Wow, what was I thinking? I thought becoming a firefighter was supposed to be glorious, glamorous, sexy, heroic, and here I was, with a bucket, mop and toothbrush in my hand scrubbing urinals and toilets! In addition, my Captain made it clear that he would be back to examine my work so I should pay attention to the details.

Well, I guess I did okay. Almost 40 years later I managed to clean enough bathrooms and make enough good decisions to earn me three Chief Officer positions. I say that, to bring to light that every job we do in the fire service is vital and important to the success of the organization. If you pay attention to detail on the small assignments like the cleaning, then it is almost a guarantee that the bigger tasks will be handled as well. Paying attention to detail and having pride in ALL work is an honorable trait.

#3. How to act at the Fire Station with co-workers

Learn to work and play well with others.

Many of us didn't know it when we were sworn into our departments that our lives were about to change forever. For me, this realization meant:

- ❖ I would now be away from my wife and children and home for a complete 24 hours every third day.
- ❖ I would be sleeping on a single bunk bed alone, not my California king.
- ❖ I would have a small locker to keep my uniforms and miscellaneous items in; not the large walk-in closet like at home.
- ❖ I would have to provide for my own meals, or pitch in funds for every meal. Not just open my fridge and get something out.

❖ I would be living in close proximity with three or more people depending on if it was a single or multiple unit station (could have up to 20).

❖ I would be listening to my co-workers "unloading" all their personal and work issues, causing undo stress, even to the point of physical confrontations.

Having said all that, when you become a professional firefighter, you quickly become aware of these things and become accustomed to living and working in that environment. (For some, it takes longer to adjust than others—some never do).

My suggestion is to build stable relationships with everyone you are assigned with. You never want to have to ask yourself, "Will Gary be there to get me out if I'm trapped?" Or, "Will Ray bail off the line when I'm running the nozzle because we may have had a fight/disagreement at the station earlier that day?" These thoughts and or events should not be taking place. If you do have differences with someone on your shift, sit down and get it out in the open and resolve it immediately. These work relationships are critical to the overall mission of your department and for the safety of all.

To Do: If there is a problem or tension, ask yourself:
1. What happened to start this off?
2. How much was fueled by me?
3. Set a time to discuss the issue(s) with your co-worker.
4. Come to an agreement and resolve the problem.
5. Be humble while doing so.
6. Always shake hands as a gesture of solidarity.

EPHESIANS 4:26, 27: *In your anger do not sin. Do not let the sun go down while you are still angry, and do not give the devil a foothold.*

A Prayer: *Help me, Lord, to control my anger, both at fires and around the Firehouse, that I might not sin against you or destroy my testimony.*

Men and Women on the Job: Not Weird, Just Different

With more women joining the fire service, men must be especially aware that your conversations should never cross that line

3

of being crude or have any sexual overtones. In years past there would be all men stations and it would sometimes appear that the station was just an extension of the college dorm or frat house with the language being used and the sexual/promiscuous material strewn about as well as XXX rated videos being played on living quarters televisions.

This behavior in all firefighters must stop now! I can tell you first hand that this kind of behavior is destructive and will cause permanent damage to everyone in the department if it continues.

You should be talking to your female partner firefighters with respect, as if she were your wife, mother, or sister. This also holds true for women in the fire service. We don't hear as much reprimanding of women for sexual harassment, but there is still enough. I would strongly recommend that you, through your department, become informed and educated by attending programs such as **Prevention of Sexual Harassment in the Workplace Training** and **Sensitivity Training**. This training will help everyone to understand each other's role within the department.

If you are married, or in a relationship with a significant other, I would strongly suggest that you tell your spouse or significant other about the people that you work with, especially those of the opposite sex. Some spouses or partners may have a jealous nature in them so it is important to let them know about the people with whom you are spending a third (or more) of your life living and working with.

In addition, I would also make it a point to introduce your spouse or significant other to all of your co-workers, both male and female. This way, they will not be wondering all the time what that person looks like and how they are as a person. Being transparent is the best way to live in the fire service today.

Recommended Checkpoints – Ask Yourself:

1. Would I talk to my spouse or significant other the way I do to my co-workers?
2. Would my mother and children be pleased with me in how I act and talk with my co-workers, especially when we are separate from the group?
3. Am I open and honest with my spouse or significant other?
4. Is there anything I can be doing at work that will strengthen the respect my co-workers have for me?

If you take a few minutes before every shift starts and ask these simple questions with your answers, you will be amazed how much better your day will go because you will be in command of yourself and be accountable.

#4. How to act at home

Some would ask, "What do you mean, how to act at home?" Well, you know how it goes. Some firefighters 'act a fool' around the fire station and we sure hope that they don't act the same way at home.

At home you are expected to be respectful to your spouse or significant other and your children. You are always being looked up to because not only are you the dad or mom, but being a professional firefighter also brings additional responsibilities. Are you acting out of character, e.g., drinking too much alcohol and acting loud or maybe getting angry with family members making everyone anxious and scared? This behavior happens too often, but must stop now!

Watching sexually explicit movies or television programs is not a good character trait, especially if you have children at home and they may see what you are watching. This can be a sign of sexual addiction or leading to it. If you smoke or chew tobacco, that will not provide your children with a healthy environment or the proper self-image you want for them. They look up to you and you wouldn't want to think back and realize they do it because they saw you do it. This is especially true since your work involves saving people's lives who were involved in drunken driving crashes for example. You must lead by example!

Children are taught at school that smoking, drinking alcohol, taking drugs, and looking at sexually explicit material are not healthy for anyone. So, if you are acting out at home with any of these vices, you are not creating a healthy and respectful family environment. These behaviors can be passed down generationally with dire consequences. Early illness and even death can result.

When you are off duty and at home ask yourself these questions:

1. Would I be drinking alcohol, chewing tobacco, or viewing sexually explicit media while I was conducting a tour of the station for a group of our neighborhood citizens?
2. Would I be yelling at my spouse or significant other or children if my grandparents were standing next to me?
3. Would I be cursing or talking foul about a neighbor if that neighbor was standing in front of me and my family?

These are simple questions to basic situations. All of them occur on a daily basis. If you are a professional firefighter, you should be able to answer "No" to each one of the questions. How you act at home carries over to how you will be acting at the station and vice versa. You have to set your personal guidelines and live by them daily.

James 5, 6: *How great a fire is set ablaze by such a small fire? And the tongue is a Fire, a world of unrighteousness. The tongue is set among our members, staining the whole body, setting on fire the entire course of life, and set on fire by hell.*

A PRAYER: *Lord, remind me to think before I speak. Give me control over my mouth and the things I say.*

#5. How to act when you are out in public

In reality, this topic shouldn't even have to be discussed, however there have been too many instances where firefighters both on duty and dressed in their department uniform, or off duty and wearing their department's crest on their t-shirt or jacket, have been acting in such a way that is not in the best interest of integrity to themselves or their department.

I have witnessed this first hand. A group of firefighters while out on a detail with the engine, stop for lunch at their favorite burger place. While sitting next to a group of young women, they start to make comments of how cute or sexy they are and the conversation leads to sharing cell phone numbers, which then turns into texting and even sexting in some cases. This is not acceptable behavior.

This scenario occurs way too often today and needs to stop! When you are sworn in as a professional firefighter in your community, you are saying, "I will act in accordance with respectful professionalism." You have now become an ambassador of that organization. When people see you out in public, and you are wearing the city's name on your person, you become accountable for all your actions. If you act out inappropriately, you will be called on it for sure. Instead of worrying about how you will defend your actions, just do the right thing and choose wisely. Be professional!

Think about the following when you are out with the public:

- I am an ambassador to my department and the city. Am I acting as a professional?
- Will my family be proud of how I carry myself? Am I a mentor to children?
- I am accountable for everything I say and do.
- I will be held accountable and be disciplined if I choose improperly.
- What would my family think of me if they saw me out in public with my co-workers when I'm off duty? Would they be proud to say "Hey, that's my dad/husband/mom/wife"? Isn't he/she great? We love him/her."

Make the right choices and your success will continue forever!

#6. Socializing at the Fire Station on and off duty

Once you become part of a firefighting family, you are part of it for life. Your comrades become an extension of your immediate biological family. You know that when they are needed for anything, they are there for you. This is a special blessing from God. There are few other professions whose members provide for this kind of care and understanding for each other.

People ask us, "How can you be a firefighter and do what you do?" To them I say, "We do it with love because we are family, helping each other through each day." Because of this bond, you don't want to do anything that will damage your relationships. Do the right thing!

Do's
1. Always be kind and act respectable.
2. Talk about your kids and sports.

3. Talk about school and what fire science classes you are taking.
4. Share family stories that are funny.
5. Talk about your hobbies and what you are doing now.
6. Share any good news that affects you or your family.
7. Ask advice on any topics that are mainstream.
8. Be happy!
9. Share your thoughts on the Word of God!
10. Strive to be a peacekeeper.

Don'ts
1. Absolutely no sexual overtones or innuendos during your casual conversation.
2. Do not make any negative comments about someone's weight or looks.
3. Shy away from talking about money and politics.
4. Do not take anything said for granted. Always go to the source for clarification.
5. Do not get verbally angry or abusive.
6. Do not use foul language.
7. Do not purposefully hurt someone's feelings.
8. Do not act out in a sexual manner including your actions or behavior.

#7. Using fire station and personal computers on and off duty

I know that when computers started being issued to our departments our bosses were excited because we all would now be able to write organized reports, build spreadsheets, develop presentations, and become "statistic gathering machines." All the things that go on during daily, monthly, yearly activities would be compiled and used to build a case for all new programs needed to successfully operate our departments.

When it came to budget preparation, the computer was a great tool. The software we had would provide for charts, graphs, text, all in various colors even. What a great administrative tool! Computers became great tools for reporting emergency responses, typing memos, preparing budgets, and keeping an inventory of our tools and equipment.

Well, that being said, managers at the time had no idea what impact the Internet would have on us all. The Internet has certainly provided us all with a personal connection to the world's information; and all from the privacy and comfort of your home or office.

This was going to make all of our lives so much better. We would be able to access pictures, videos, and read about any topic. I remember when Internet explorer was the only search engine, and dial up from a phone line using AOL (America On-Line) became our access point to the World Wide Web.

We were astonished how we could type a few words in the browser/URL space and push <Enter> and a plethora of information would pop up on our desired topic. Any information with those keywords in it, by anybody who had uploaded that information, would come up (pictures, graphs, video, written documents, etc.

I say all that as a short history lesson for anyone that did not go through that time frame of "Computer 101" in the field. For us old timers, we had OJT (On the Job Training) to learn how to operate the computers. I also say that as a lead in to discuss how we became addicted to accessing the World Wide Web once we knew how. It was like being a kid in the candy store. Everything available to us with just a few pushes of the buttons.

As you know now, one problem that arose out of having computers was the access to pornographic material in the fire stations via the Internet. There was more "information" than anyone could fathom. What most users didn't know was that the URL you went to was being kept in the history log on the computer's hard drive. That history has the time and date when the site was accessed, along with the user password ID for the individual using the computer at that time.

Fire department officers running shifts were some of the first personnel to be trained on the use of the computers and some of the first to explore the Internet. It wasn't long after the start of computers in the fire house that we saw more and more officers— and firefighters—accessing pornographic websites; initially it usually involved downloading and displaying pictures and then evolved into videos. Who would have thought that so many of our firefighters around the nation would become so addicted to on-line porn?

Unfortunately, hundreds of firefighters have been subjected to disciplinary actions, including termination for accessing pornographic material while on duty.

Do Not ever use a department issued computer of any kind including, desk top, laptop, iPad, iPhone, Blackberry, tablet, etc., to look at pornographic material of any kind. This can most likely get you fired today. It can even get you arrested and sentenced to a prison term if you have pornographic material of anyone under the age of 18.

Do Not use your personal desk top PC, smartphone, iPad, tablet, laptop etc., to take and/or send naked pictures of yourself or co-workers.

Do Not download any material that contains photographs of any individual that can be considered to be under the age of 18 years old by law enforcement. They will charge you with child pornography. You don't want to have to deal with federal criminal charges for possession of child pornography. It has been customary that those who are convicted on such charges will receive 5 to 20 years in a federal prison. This is not something you and your loved ones want to live through and with.

This is why I talk about moral aptitude and maintaining a high standard of both moral actions and ethics. Integrity must prevail. If you are a believer in the "Word" you already know that God is never pleased with immorality. He will "put it in your life" that you will know He isn't happy with your choices. That, I can tell you, is not how you want to know God.

Do work with computers. Use them for all your work assignments. These tools are a gift to complete projects that in the past would not have been done as efficiently and effectively. We are blessed to have the software and hardware that helps us keep our departments running smooth and effective.

Do use your personal computers of all types for what is good in life. We are blessed to have the instant capabilities today to: video chat with a loved one overseas serving in a war zone; take and send fun family photos and videos instantly using social media apps; send text messages; and watch movies and TV programs from our hand held devices. These are all gifts. Use them wisely.

#8. When you stop to shop or go to lunch on or off duty

Those "OOPS" moments

I bet as soon as you read this title, it immediately brought up a past situation that you remember happening while you were out somewhere. Perhaps you were having lunch or stopped by a famous coffee shop and something happened that made you say, "OOPS"! This moment could have been prompted by something that almost happened or that actually happened.

The good thing for us is that an "OOPS" moment will usually only bring an embarrassing moment where your face turns red, we say, "Oh I'm sorry", and we go on about our business. Listed below are a few Dos and Don'ts to think over.

Don't - Smoke or use spit tobacco, especially spitting in a cup or bottle. This includes while you are driving in your vehicle. Citizens, especially today, do not expect professional firefighters to be smoking and dipping. We have all known for many years now just how much of a health hazard tobacco use is and how it contributes to cancer and other illnesses all over the world.

Ask yourself, "Would I be a good role model for children if they saw me smoking in our assigned apparatus?" Or in your personal vehicle, which undoubtedly will have a Firefighter's Maltese Cross insignia displayed on your window. Or you may be wearing a t-shirt that has your city's name and company crest on it. Children and parents are pretty smart nowadays!

Don't - Use foul or coarse language. If you are shopping for dinner on your way back to the station and one of you gets upset and says something like "f'- that" and someone hears you in the aisle, what do you think they will think about you as a firefighter in their city? This would be one of those "OOPS" moments I'm talking about.

You turn to that person that you offended and say, "I'm sorry I shouldn't have said that," and be sincere. Everyone makes mistakes.

Take responsibility and you will feel better, and your crew and department will save face. Less chance your chief will receive a call from that citizen in the morning if you "nip it in the bud."

Don't make any negative gestures, e.g., the "middle finger salute", to anyone while you are driving down the road. You already know that "all eyes" are on us as soon as we leave the station. Your community members are proud of you, and they claim you as "their firefighters." Make them, your families, and your department proud.

Don't make an inappropriate gesture to a very attractive woman, or stop next to her car and look down at her from your apparatus seat high above to see how she is dressed. This will get you into one of those "OOPS" moments with her, and more importantly with the boss. These situations—and many more like them—happen, but we shouldn't let them.

Don't act like you are better than others, or entitled. We are blessed to be firefighters, not more blessed than others because we are firefighters.

Do behave in a humble manner! Everyone already admires firefighters; it is not necessary to show off in any way.

Do be kind. Open doors for those walking in and out of the store with you. You never know who that person could be. It could be the chief's wife or daughter, a relative to the mayor or city manager or it could also be family to your fire house family. You don't want to have to explain one of those "OOPS" moments to any of them, right?

You may be saying, "Come on chief, why be so strict?" I say, we are held to a higher standard because we said that we would. We can't just "talk the talk", we have to "walk the talk." Respect is earned not given!

#9. Talking on your personal or station house phone while on or off duty

On or off duty at the fire station means – you can either be on duty assignment, or be off duty and just stopped by to drop something off or chat and leaving out again soon. Like I had mentioned before, once you become a member of a department, you become part of that department's family. That alone has its own dynamics (We will discuss this in more detail later).

Don't stop by the fire station to conduct your personal business. The "house phone" in the fire station is there for fire department business, and to receive calls from family members when you are on duty.

You are putting your career in jeopardy when you conduct business from which you derive money, e.g., calling clients or suppliers for your contracting business, while using city phones. This is a conflict of interest and crosses the line of ethical behavior expected of municipal employees.

Don't use the "house phone" for any personal calls that you wouldn't want your spouse or significant other or your children to hear. In every fire station the "walls have ears". You can be assured that what you are saying on the phone, no matter if it is completely legitimate or not, will be heard by someone in the station and then regurgitated to others. When it is all said and done, what you were talking about went from a nice topic, to a sleazy unethical topic; or from nonsexual to sexual, etc.

Do use your own phone for personal and private business calls. This is the best course of action. Period.

Use your personal car or truck for private conversations if you are on the road, and of course home is the most secure place. Keep your personal life on the phone just that, personal!

#10. Practical Jokes and "horseplay" at the Fire Station

I know for a fact that this topic already has you smiling and laughing thinking back as recently as last shift perhaps on a practical joke that someone pulled on someone else at the station. This practical joking also known as hazing, in some instances, occurs on a regular basis. It could be done just because you know that your co-worker has a good sense of humor, or not so much perhaps, and everyone (except him) enjoys watching him get angry the more others laugh. I can remember the shaving cream in my boots, a snake or two in the bunk, or something slimy inside the rim of my helmet.

As much as these seem to provide for some entertainment, there are some practical jokes, or hazing of rookies for example that can be devastating to one's career, either as the maker or receiver.

I can remember in 2012 when a company officer at a fire station in Georgia orchestrated a prank to scare a group of rookies sitting in the day room. The stunt had an outsider come in through a back stairway to the living area, pull out a gun and hold a rookie firefighter hostage to the floor and tell him not to move or he would kill him. Well, I bet you know how that ended up for all who were "in on it", especially the officer! That can be one of those "career limiting or ending" moves.

You may be saying, "Chief, what's the big deal?" The big deal is that when we start disrespecting "our own", we lose respect for ourselves and our integrity diminishes. Here are a few Dos and Don'ts to ponder over:

Don't plan, be a part of, or execute any practical jokes. What may be funny to you may not be funny to another firefighter on your crew. People's lives and jobs are on the line every day. Don't add to the stress by playing practical jokes too.

Do treat all your brothers and sisters in the fire service with ultimate respect, whether they just came on the job, or are ready to retire. Help one another with all matters pertinent to good work ethics and a positive environment (In other words, be kind and use common sense).

Do look out for each other at all times. This encompasses many addictive behaviors that can cause a brother or sister firefighter to "fall from grace" personally or professionally such as:

- Alcohol or substance abuse
- Viewing pornography on the Internet
- Domestic violence towards a spouse or significant other or child
- Gambling

As a firefighter, you have been given a special gift by God, and that is to be there for each other. Stopping a situation from happening is as heroic as knocking down a room fire with a victim rescue. Do the right thing!

#11. Dress code when on or off duty

This topic should be easy enough to figure out. When reporting for duty, you will be following the departments SOG's or SOP's for uniform wear. Many departments now require that personnel change into their departmental uniform upon arriving at the station as a means of preventing personnel from "taking stuff home", i.e., transferring contaminants from the fire station to their homes via their uniforms. (This practice, as well as only laundering uniforms at the fire station, is worthy of following even if they are not an official SOG for your department).

While on duty, whether in uniform or in workout clothing for physical training, keep all body parts covered as to not be suggestive in a sensual way. I'm talking about no one walking around in undergarments or shirtless for men or just bras for women. You never know when a member of the public may stop at your station to ask for directions or ask that their child be given a chance to see the fire trucks. Nor do you know when a spouse or significant other of one of the on-duty members will stop by the station for...whatever the reason. Do you really want to answer questions regarding why you or other crew members were on duty in various stages of undress?

An important part of your structural firefighting protective ensemble, aka, your bunker gear, is the clothing underneath of it. Except when engaging in physical training, you should be wearing your approved station uniform so that you have that second layer of protection. (Never put on your structural protective clothing over workout clothing made with synthetic fabrics as these can melt to your skin under your turnout gear if the temperature around you gets high enough). Following these simple rules will keep everyone on the same page. The safe page!

I would be remiss if I didn't mention again that when you are a community firefighter, you become known as such. That means that whether or not you are wearing your department colors or not when you are off duty, you share that extra responsibility to represent your community as that ambassador we mentioned earlier. Don't forget, someone is always watching and listening to you no matter where you are. As long as you are acting respectfully, there should be nothing to worry about.

#12. Sex in the Fire Station

I know that your eyes opened wider when you reached this topic. But for real, you knew that I would be addressing it since we have had so many incidents over the years where this topic was the root cause for many infractions.

From as far back as I can remember, there have been stories about firefighters having sex in their fire stations. Wives, girlfriends, or newly met friends would stop by to bring lunch or dinner and, well, they stayed a little while longer than expected.

We first saw it on the big screen in the movie, *Back Draft*, where the rookie (Who was also the Captain's brother) was depicted having sex with a young lady on the hose bed of his engine in the station. If you took your spouse or significant other at the time to see that movie, or *Ladder 49* (which had a similar scene), did you not find yourself being asked these questions:

"Well honey does this actually go on?"

"Does it go on in your station?"

A few years passed and we saw the FX mini-series, *Rescue Me*, depicting New York City firefighters working and living their lives out in day to day activities, on and off duty. This series did not do any justice for the fire service in the areas of morality, or being kind for that matter. What it did, was to show how "out of control" firefighters can be. The show's protagonist, Tommy Gavin (portrayed by Denis Leary), was a senior firefighter who personified how firefighters can be out of control alcoholics, prescription and street drug users, and sex addicts of various levels on TV week after week.

The major issue I had with this portrayal was that it was made for TV/movies, and that the general public would start to program their minds that all firefighters act this way, including their own community's firefighters. Not good for our self-image. The sad part is that there are many firefighters who are inflicted by these conditions, but in no way all of them. People started asking me;

16

"Chief, does this really go on?" I wish I could have said no, but the reality is, it does.

We do not assume that the behavior depicted on *Rescue Me* and the latest TV series, *Chicago Fire*, are the signature for all fire departments across the country. What it does say is, enough of this activity has taken place at one time or another in fire houses that movie producers and directors want to add it to their story line. (They know that sex sells.)

I can honestly say that a lot of guys I worked with in the North had issues with alcohol, drug use, and sex addictions of various types. When I moved South, I saw and dealt with it there also. As chief, I would counsel and assist my firefighters through various difficulties that stemmed from these types of addictions.

As I toured and taught firefighting across the United States and Canada as well as internationally, I saw it there also, from coast to coast. No department can escape the human emotion of behavior.

There is no excuse for these behaviors, but the stress level is very high and a lot of firefighters find easing the pain of stress by acting out in a variety of different ways. It just seems that the use of alcohol, drugs, and extra-marital sexual activity are the most common. Today we are also seeing a higher number of suicides among members of our profession.

Here are a few Dos and Don'ts to think about:

Don't invite anyone to your fire station to have sex. None – Never – No How – Period! If you get caught you will most likely be terminated.

If you are married and involved with another person and think that you can just have that person over to your station to have sex, forget it. Even if you don't get caught by your company officer, the whole department will know about it that next morning, or even that night.

Remember what I said earlier, "the walls have ears and eyes". Computers and smartphones transfer information in micro-seconds. You could even find your picture or video all over the Internet and all over the world. YouTube or Twitter are used a lot for that purpose today.

Do act with moral integrity and high standards at all time. Treat yourself and your spouse or significant other with respect. Your co-workers may not outwardly judge you, but if you give them ammunition like that, you may not be held in high esteem with some.

Do ask yourself these questions if you are already having sex in your fire station, or are planning to:

- Am I breaking departmental rules and regulations?
- If I am, what is the punishment if I am caught and charged?
- Will I lose my job?
- How will I deal with the shame and peer harassment?
- If there is another person in your personal life, what will he or she think? Will you lose that person from your life, including your children?
- How guilty will you feel, and how will it affect your job performance?
- How will you earn back the respect you will lose?
- Are you leading by example as a serious professional?
- How will you explain your violation to family? (Word will get to them you know.)

Be professional and make the right choices from the start. Be morally courageous! This is not one of those "oops" moments!

#13. Personal interactions with co-workers

Do's and Don'ts
Don't let your co-workers/friends drive under any influences
Don't provoke anyone to do anything immoral or illegal
Don't be nosey with someone else's relationships
Don't become jealous for any reason
Do build solid and long lasting relationships
Do be someone's support or even their "rock" if needed.
Do be kind in your friendships
Do be patient
Do build trust together
Do share in the Word

#14. Use of departmental equipment

Do's and Don'ts
Don't ever take a piece of equipment off a truck and take it home to use it on your own home projects, e.g., a chain saw.
Don't miss a check out of your truck's equipment
Don't abuse any of your equipment or the equipment of others. This includes personal protective gear. Too often a person's turnout gear has been the target of a practical joker and this practice must stop. Our protective gear is too important for fun and games.
Do keep all your equipment clean and functional
Do treat all your equipment and apparatus like it is your own
Do let your officer know if there is anything wrong with your equipment
Do follow all your SOG's on tool and equipment usage

#15. Use of sexual innuendos or overtones at the station

Do's and Don'ts
Don't use any language that can be considered offensive by people such as your spouse, significant other, or other family members.
Do at any time, stay away from any verbiage during any discussions with your co-workers or others that has sexual innuendos or overtones, such as, "Wow, Julie, you looked really hot last night when I saw you."
Do always act respectable and respectful

#16. How to address senior leadership in your department

A senior member is any fire department member that is of higher rank than you from Lieutenant to Chief of Department.

Don't shun an officer when you are addressed by him or her. That will be disrespectful and probably not sit well with him or her.

Don't argue with an officer. The last thing you want is to be reprimanded by your company officer. We all have opinions and we can share the information calmly.

Do always acknowledge an officer verbally by his or her rank, e.g., "Good afternoon Chief" or "Good morning Captain"; or responding with, "Yes Sir", or "No Sir" when asked a question. (Some women find the term, Ma'am, as in "Yes, Ma'am", to be offensive. With women officers a better phrase to use would be "Yes, Chief" or "No Captain.")

Do when you have a difference in opinion, always meet to discuss the issue in private.

#17. When you are at headquarters for a meeting

Do's and Don'ts
Don't be disrespectful in any way.

Don't make any verbal comments that could be misconstrued as a sexual innuendo or overtones. This could also be considered sexual harassment.

Don't use cuss words or foul language.

Do be on time – Be neat and clean from head to toe.

Do be in the proper uniform.

Do be on your best behavior.

Do address everyone as sir or ma'am or by their rank, etc.

Do be prepared to answer any questions from an officer, be polite.

#18. When driving the Chief's car

Do's and Don'ts
Don't ever park in front of a fire hydrant

Don't ever use your emergency lights or siren unless you are responding to an emergency.

Don't try and show off by riding by friend's homes or your house with the chief's car.

Do realize this is your chance to show how mature and responsible you are.

Do obey the speed limit.

Do use directional signals.

Do acknowledge those who may wave or say hello to you.

Do obey all traffic laws. People are watching you.

#19. Driving apparatus – emergency and non-emergency

Do's and Don'ts

Don't break any traffic laws, especially speeding (both emergency and non-emergency). We can't be effective if we don't make it to the scene.

Don't use your lights and siren unless required, or dictated by your response; if you are going to the market, no lights or siren; if you are responding to a fire, use both; if you are conducting hydrant testing, lights on only to act as a warning to drivers that you are working in place.

Don't show off or show out while driving in the community. No getting too close to the car in front of you because your friend is driving it, or if you see an attractive woman.

Do always drive in accordance with your department's SOG's and your training.

Do obey all traffic laws, especially what you are to do when approaching intersections, stop signs, and traffic lights.

Do always keep your apparatus clean.

Do be professional at all times while in operation.

Do be courteous at all times. Citizens are taxpayers, who contribute to your salary and the purchase of our apparatus.

#20. Taking apparatus to the Supermarket, Home Repair Store, etc.

Do's and Don'ts

Don't block any parking spaces if you are at the store or mall on a detail. The public gets a little possessive of their spaces and don't think a fire truck, not working an emergency should be there hanging out and blocking spaces for customers. This happens a lot. Your crew may be in the store also, but I would suggest putting the truck away from the general parking spaces but close enough to get out front if you receive a call to respond, where the crew can meet you out front.

Don't act out in any inappropriate way. Remember, all eyes are on you, especially the children!

Do act respectful to all citizens that you may come in contact with while you are positioning your apparatus in the parking lot of your store.

Do be ready to answer questions from the public, such as; "Is there an emergency or fire?" "No ma'am, we are just stopping for supplies for the station." Smile while you respond. Not everyone of the public thinks it's OK to take your fire engine to the grocery store for lunch or dinner supplies, being polite helps.

#21. Personal hygiene and overall cleanliness

Webster dictionary describes hygiene as: *Being healthy – A system of principals for preserving health and cleanliness.*

We all know how important it is that we keep ourselves healthy and clean. Not only is it a department requirement, but also a professional requirement for all firefighters.

We all have worked with someone who may not have taken that concept to heart, and may have been on the edge of both. It is in all our best interest that we maintain this standard as one of those high standards. After all, we are professionals and our customers expect us to show up that way!

Don't show up for duty unshaven with your uniform wrinkled
Don't be offensive to your co-workers by how you smell
Don't leave your personal mess for someone else to clean up
Don't leave your food and dishes out for someone else to clean
Don't leave trash in your apparatus
Do report for duty clean and ready to handle your business
Do make sure your hair on your head and face meet department regs.
Do ensure your uniform is clean and pressed, shoes shined
Do ensure your hands are clean and ready for gloves
Do brush your teeth and use mouthwash

#22. Work and Dress Uniforms

In my introduction you see what I noted about what a uniform is: "A Uniform reminds you that *you are* in fact what you are wearing". Saying that, should always remind us how much it means to us and to those we serve, just what a blessing it is to be a firefighter.

Do's and Don'ts – Dress Uniforms
Don't disrespect your dress uniform by not wearing it clean, pressed, and complete as stated above.
Do wear the Class 'A' Uniform with pride; it always makes us feel proud. Our Class A dress uniform allows us to display our rank in the form of stripes on our sleeves, 1 stripe for Lieutenant, 2 for Captain, 3 for Division or Assistant Chief, 4 for Deputy Chief, and 5 stripes for Chief of Department. Most departments also display the years of service by placing one sewn on Maltese Cross for each 5 years served. In addition, we display our badge, name tag, and all ribbons/commendations of awards on our chest. On the lapels some will wear their bugle rank insignia. Your ensemble should be complete with hat, dress shirt and tie, coat, dress slacks, dark socks and shined shoes.

The Work Uniform has been made extremely durable over the last 10 years, especially if you are wearing a Nomex work uniform shirt and pants. They hold up to abrasiveness, tear resistant, and can withstand higher heat temperatures compared to the polyester and cotton blends worn in the past. They are wrinkle free if you take them out of the dryer on time.

Do's and Don'ts – Work Uniforms
Do keep your work uniform clean at all times, especially between EMS responses. Most department's infectious disease control policy require the changing and or washing of uniforms if any contaminants were present.
Don't bring your work uniform home and place it in your home personal washer and dryer machines. You never know for sure what sort of contaminants you may have picked up on your uniform over a 24-hour period of time. Most departments now have washing machine extractors and dryers at each station so you can do it there.
Don't wear your department uniform if you are working another part time department or ambulance company job. Each department or company should supply their own uniforms.

#23. Use of alcohol and/or drugs on or off duty

It's never been a hidden secret that firefighters may on occasion get together and have a social drink or two after a shift or when they are off duty to celebrate a birthday, anniversary, promotion, engagement, etc. This being said, we also know that there have been many bad choices made by a few to drink heavy the night before their morning shift starts and they are still considered to be over the legal limit, or actually drink while they are on duty. We also have seen over the years that our firefighters are becoming addicted to prescription pain medication and some using illegal drugs such as marijuana and cocaine. The use of any of these substances can become habit forming and addictive.

It almost sounds insane that firefighters would show up with a high alcohol blood count, or still high from drug use either from prescription meds or illegal drugs. We saw this depicted in 'Back Draft', Ladder 49', 'Rescue Me', and 'Chicago Fire'. When we see those firefighters acting out of control, or see a behavior that is not representative of a professional firefighter we ask "What is going on here?"

When you ask those firefighters why, you get many reasons, or excuses like; I'm under so much stress at home, financial problems, going through a divorce, my girlfriend cheated on me, my boyfriend treats me bad, I'm living with shame I can't take anymore. For all these issues, they try and reduce the pain by drinking or using one kind of drug or another. These symptoms occur in many other work professionals, however, they are not responsible for life saving initiatives. When you are a firefighter on duty and assigned any position, you need to be 100% on task mentally, emotionally, morally, and physically in order to perform your duties in saving lives and property. Being under the influence of any altering substance is unacceptable. If you are involved in this behavioral pattern and activity, I would strongly suggest you seek assistance in house or outside your workplace before something very bad happens. You can prevent it. Get it together now!

#24. Gambling at the Fire Station on or off duty

I have to admit that I am not an expert at this topic however I do know enough that it is not an activity that is sanctioned and supported by your fire department senior staff.

Over my fire service career, I saw gambling occur in fire stations in the form of football, baseball, basketball, and even NASCAR racing boards. This type of gambling can start off and appear to be a friendly game of chance. Of course anytime winning or losing any amounts of money is in play, the human behaviors show up also. I have seen bets ranging from $1 to $500 bet on a sporting event. The weekend at fire houses around the country are pretty much dedicated to watching sports and eating while being on the ready to respond to calls for service.

Even though it seems like just friendly bets, when someone loses $500 to $1000 on a football game bet for example, the stress level is increased dramatically. I have heard verbal arguments get out of control that have led to physical confrontations which will only lead to one of those 'career limiting or ending moves'. Some departments will not tolerate any form of violence as acceptable and you could lose your job for fighting/assaulting another member on duty. I would suggest that if you and your crew members do gamble in house, I would think about changing that to not doing it. If you must compete, make it something like; if your team wins, I'll handle the food or wash the dishes etc. The least money lost the better. Your spouses and significant others will be happier also.

#25. Pornography at the Fire Station

I know you may be saying, "Alright Chief, enough with the pornography prevention lessons!" Well I wish I didn't feel compelled to cover so many topics relating to it, but unfortunately it is the #1 vice that challenges our firefighters to remain morally sound and morally courageous while on duty. In my previous section involving computer usage at the fire station, we see how dangerous it is having access to the internet. It is so easy today to get online and access free porn sites. In a matter of a couple of seconds, you can be up and viewing material that is damaging to your moral core and literally take you out of your job.

Back in the days, 1975 circa, you would see a plethora of Playboy, Hustler, and other pornographic material lying around the fire house. This was in a time that porn was not considered as immoral as it has become. It has become so destructive, that department management had to have legal departments write special orders, directives, and operational memorandums on the non-access, or keeping of pornographic material in print or electronically via a VHS tape, CD, DVD and of course the most easily accessed, internet porn.

Those firefighters that started using station computers for porn found themselves disciplined, and some even terminated. Others said "Well I'll just bring in my own laptop, or now the iPhone, or iPad and access it that way. Some governments won't allow their members to bring in personal computer equipment and only a cell phone with the instructions that if you are caught viewing pornography you will be disciplined in accordance with department policy. If you are a Christian, I would suggest reading through the Bible and you will see over 100 verses that discount and deplore sexual immorality which this porn would fall under. Your wife/husband, girlfriend/boyfriend and other family members deserve more from us. Real intimacy, not false intimacy, "Take it from a Chief who knows."

Thessalonian 4:3: For this is God's will, your sanctification: that you abstain from sexual immorality.

#26. Video cam usage at the Fire Station on and off duty

Well folks, I wish I didn't have to even list this topic but unfortunately I have to. I remember when the monitor mounted video cams first came out. Many people were very excited, others couldn't figure out how to use it or set it up. You needed to upload a software CD, hook up cables and configure your computer whether desktop or laptop to get it to work. The only way you could use it is if the other person you were talking with had one also and you would then have to invite and accept each other to get a connection. Like anything new in technology, it took a while before it became so easy and actually integrated into our computers of all kinds, (desktops, laptops, iPhones, cell phone/PD's, iPads, where now the camera is built into the devices and already configured so when your unit is turned on, you are video cam ready to voice/video real time chat with anyone in the world that has a video cam on their system.

Now you know what started happening when everyone realized that they could be sitting at their desk, on their bed, on the couch, in a chair, in the car, on a bus, train, plane, anywhere in the fire house and be able to 'Face Time' or 'Video Chat' with your family, friends, extended circle of friends, and complete strangers you meet in Yahoo Chat rooms, or on Facebook, etc.

All this easy accessibility is great if you keep everything in line with good moral behavior and good ethical behavior. The problems come in when someone decides to drop their moral guard and start viewing someone and talking to them while he or she is disrobing and beyond. This occurs a lot nowadays in fire houses around the country. Unfortunately, Chief's spend a lot of their day with personnel directors and legal council meeting to deal with these issues.

Take it from a Chief that knows firsthand. If you are doing this at the station or home, STOP! This can become a sexual addictive behavior that will stifle your professional and personal growth in so many ways. Seek assistance if you need to, but stop now!

#27. Smart phone use for texting/sexting

Before we actually had such easy access to 'video cam' or 'face time' with our smart phones, we all relied on using our hand held cell phones to text a message to someone. I remember the first time I could send someone a text message from typing into my cell phone/blackberry and have them send me an almost instant reply. I thought this was amazing and could be fun also. Well it became a great tool for us multi-taskers, where we wouldn't have to spend extra time actually talking on the phone with someone if we just needed some basic info at any time or just sending trivial info to a friend or colleague.

This became the fad, and 'must have' tool for everyone, even the teenagers that could have cell phones.

What everyone quickly realized was that you could say just about anything you wanted to your co-worker or friend or family member, when I say anything, well I mean some things that are considered immoral and downright nasty, sexually explicit in all aspects. You could say things now to someone else that you would never say in person unless you were already in an approved intimate relationship like your wife/husband.

This texting became what is now known as 'sexting'! Oh my, it got so out of control all over the world. In the U.S. we have political figures that think sexting a picture of themselves naked, or a picture of their penis to a woman they barely know was an OK thing to do. Well guess what Senator or Congressman, it wasn't and you got called out on it.

So many marriages and other relationships have been damaged or destroyed by the use of smart phone sexting. Talking dirty, like cyber-sex, using your phone for video chat while sexting is running rampart in fire houses today. If you are conducting yourself like this while on duty, you will most likely be caught and called out on it and face discipline, or your significant other may find out and your relationship goes by the wayside. If this is occurring to you or with one of your crew members, please have them stop now and seek alternatives like seeking counseling from your pastor or a counselor. This behavior is addictive. Sex addictions come in all forms.

#28. Picture taking at the Fire Station

This is a topic that has had some play around the country over the past several years. You wouldn't think that taking a few pictures of outside and inside the station, or of your fire apparatus, even of your mascot Sparky the Fire Dog would cause any problems for you at the station.

Well, it wouldn't, as long as the pictures were just of those individual items and no human enhancements. I think you get my point. If your department has never had an incident where a good natured department member either personally, or had a visitor come in and took pictures of themselves or others that were inappropriate in front of your apparatus, like a group of women in skimpy bikini's which will be used in an upcoming wall calendar to help raise money for a particular cause, or a group of guys without shirts and oiled down for use in a calendar, then you are one of the fortunate ones.

We have even seen where naked pictures were found of non-department members inside fire apparatus, or in a crew room, etc. I know you get the message on this one.

This offense is not taken lightly by the chief, city manager, mayor, city council members, your family members, and of course the tax paying community citizen.

When these images show up on Social Media platforms as an example, and then an investigation ensues, and usually someone will come out with the info needed to put an end to the case.

The good natured member, or members, will be reprimanded, and could be terminated. In addition, the station officer that had nothing to do with it, or even knew of it could be disciplined also. After all, the company officers are ultimately responsible for all their personnel while on duty.

These types of incidents are destructive to 'All' parties involved, including the house family, and personal family members. How will your wife or husband, girlfriend or boyfriend feel if you have been part of this activity? Remain morally courageous and professional at all times. When I say these things, believe me, you don't want to have to go through 'All' the aftermath. Something that started off fun and what you thought was no big deal is disastrous.

#29. Outside visitors at the Fire Station

We all know that on occasion, some of our vendors/suppliers will stop by your fire station to show you the latest technology tool, equipment, system, or service that will help you be safer and more effective at your job.

That is always appreciated. What can also happen during that visit is someone could say something or do something that is out of line which could upset both the vendor and the department member, or come across as a sexual innuendo, or even considered sexual harassment.

I am aware of cases where a vendor has said something to a female member that crossed the line, words that have sexual overtones that may be taken as asking for an encounter of sorts. During my career, I often had vendors want to give us/me/department a token of their appreciation like a special pocket rescue tool, or knife, or spanner wrench, etc., if we would consider them on the upcoming bid for an item or equipment that they sell.

The first instance is sexual harassment which needs to be investigated with a conclusion, and the second is a valid case of unethical business practices of which we all need to stay clear of. An honest giving can become what some may consider a bribe of some sort. These things do happen. Stay awake and aware of what is happening around you at all times.

When in doubt, refer that vendor to the Chief's office for all business activity.

#30. Family members at the Fire House

We are all proud of what we do and where we do it. Our 'Fire House' is termed that for a specific reason, because it is our second 'Home' where we will spend more than half a lifetime. Because of the amount of time we spend at the Fire House, our families miss us and want to see us during our 24 hour shifts, especially when our children are young. They are all proud of us to, and want to see us working and even bring a friend or two to the station to see their daddy's fire station and his fire truck.

This is great for us when we are on duty; however, we have to respect our department's rules and regulations governing visits. We all know that if there is a policy or directive covering a topic, it is because something happened to someone on a visit. This could have been an injury from a slip and fall on the apparatus floor, or coming out of an apparatus. Taking it one step further, we have had instances when a wife/husband/girlfriend/boyfriend came by and stays a little too long and one thing leads to another. That could be problematic. Keep these items in mind when your family visits the station while you are on duty. If you follow department rules, all should go well and everyone has a great day.

#31. Watching TV/movies at the Fire Station

Ever since I started my career in 1975, the television and crew room has been a 'Favorite Room' for most all firefighters. Some company officers will approve watching the news in the morning during breakfast, some won't. News and sports come on during lunch time, and then off until all duties assigned have been completed for the day. Typically, this will be just before dinner is started and will continue on if there are no after dinner duties such as training, inspections, etc. By 8 PM, folks will head for the crew room to watch TV. In some stations, there is more than one big screen TV, so there could be news on one and a sports event playing on the other. The important aspect of TV usage is what you are watching. I know that X-rated programs are played, and some DVD's that can also cross that moral integrity line. I strongly recommend that you do not play anything that falls in those categories. Watch programs and movies that your wife/husband and even your children wouldn't be offended by if they walked in on y'all. Company officers are overall responsible for your actions along with you, so decide now if you want to get him/her in trouble with you. Don't forget, you will have to work with him or her for a long time after the incident passes through. Make the right choice and be morally courageous.

#32. Personal space between each other

I know this sounds lame for some of you. However, with men and women working in fire stations today, we see many sexual harassment complaints filed. Where the topic of violation of personal space, or touching while on a couch or chase lounger has become an issue. What can start off as fun; can end up in a sexual harassment law suit. Men and men, women and women, men and women sit on this furniture together so I would strongly suggest that you 'keep appropriate space' between each other. No touching in any way is the best way to prevent any issues. No arm on arms, legs on legs, hands on hands, etc. Again, you are at work, you are all professional firefighters, and you must act that way. Be morally sound.

#33. Inappropriate touching between members

This topic is a spin-off of the previous topic; however, we now see more and more intimate relationships forming between firefighters that work together. If you are in a personal relationship with your co-worker and cannot seem to be able to control your emotions from a lustful standpoint, and have to kiss and touch etc., then I would strongly suggest asking for a transfer to another shift or even company. These relationships are great, however difficult to maintain where either party doesn't get jealous, even other crew members. Make wise choices!

#34. Sexually explicit magazines of any kind

When I talk about sexually explicit material, I am talking about magazines such as Playboy, Hustler, Gent, as well as R rated Maxim as examples. We know that in today's environment, these types of publications have no place being left out in any location in the fire house. The days of having a copy of each in every toilet stall, TV room, alarm room, kitchen, and bunk rooms is over, or should be. Department policy covers this topic. And believe me, women firefighters do not want to see it out, or have to be compared to the women in them. Don't have them. That is the best choice.

#35. Male and female firefighter qualifications and performance

With more women entering the fire service, us men have to 'step up', and recognize that women firefighters, when they get on the job, had passed all the same tests as the men did. Treat your female co-workers with respect. It is time to drop the discrimination and adverse behavior towards our professional women firefighters. They are trained to do what the men do, and you may even find her saving your butt on your next fire call. Be kind and respectful!

#36. Showing respect for each other

I think that you would agree with me that shared respect for one another is a key piece of God's Word. He commands us to look after one another at all times, and treat thy neighbor as yourself. This behavior should be exemplified every day to each member of your crew at all times.

The job we do is a high risk occupation. We depend on each other's respect to get us through every incident.

Every time I have attended and or participated in a funeral service for the loss of a firefighter, I see the outpouring of respect and love for each other on the job. Hundreds of fellow firefighters will travel through all sorts of adverse conditions to attend a FIREFIGHTERS' funeral to pay their respects for a job well done, saluting the last call he or she has made to help someone in need. That's the outward show of care and respect for each other. I would like to suggest that we not wait for another funeral of a fallen brother or sister to show our respects, we should be showing it to them every shift while they are alive and well. We risk a lot to save a lot. Let us risk taking that Godly step toward grace and love shown to all those we work with every day. Tell your crew members how much you appreciate them and what they mean to you. This will make you both feel good.

#37. Starting rumors about a co-worker

We all have feelings, we are emotional beings, and when we are challenged in any way we get upset. Similar to practical jokes, starting 'false' rumors about a co-worker is inappropriate in every way. No one wants to feel left out, or laughed at for a crazy rumor that someone has just pulled out of the sky. Just, don't do it.

#38. Picture taking at the scene and sharing

I recently read headlines online where yet another firefighter medic lost his job and was personally sued for sharing pictures he had taken of an automobile fatality victim. A young girl killed in a car crash, he was one of the firefighter/medics working the scene.

He apparently, as reported, sent the pictures of the deceased young lady showing all the details of her injuries to some friends using his cell phone camera, who in turn sent them to more friends etc. etc...

Department policy was already in place and members had been advised of the policy that states, no personnel other than the department designated PIO, or accident scene officer will take pictures of any victims and any scenes for any reason and share them with others.

The family sued and won a large settlement. The firefighter/medic lost his job. Many lives were hurt in the process. Follow your department rules and regulations/directives, as well as use good moral and ethical judgment when on the job.

#39. Acting professional in all jobs

I know this topic may sound redundant, or not worthy to point out specifically, however, some firefighters think that when working a structure fire, you will be as professional as anyone can ever be. This may be true. Even with that particular job, I have seen firefighters disrespect their company officers and co-workers on the scene of a working fire. Whether you are working a structure fire or some other scene it is vital that you show respect for all those working with you.

When firefighters are out of the station teaching at schools, checking hydrants, shopping, etc., they should always act in a professional manner. There are a lot of jobs we do in the fire service, and we must conduct ourselves professionally at every one of them.

#40. How you personally act on and off duty

Did I mention the night I received a call from one of my firefighters to 'let me know' that another one of my firefighters had been dancing on a bar top and pulled his pants down to show everything he owned to everyone there!? Well yup, he did, and got thrown out of the local dance club. The police were already outside so they had to investigate the disturbance. No charges were pressed from the club owner, however our entire city and department had to now bear the 'black eye' of 'shame' that we would feel because of this ludicrous act.

The firefighter was off duty; however, many citizens at the club knew he was a local firefighter, and many of his co-workers were partying with him.

No one stepped in when he got up on the bar to stop him before he made things worse. This is one example when I say, "watch out for each other in a morally, ethical and professional way". We will live with that incident forever more. Make the better choice, don't do it. Be professional all the time!

#41. Family cluster at the Fire Station

A fire department family has a very unique bond. Unless you have been in one, you cannot know it. The family cluster provides for their own in many special ways. Things are talked about and acted on that we wouldn't deal with, with our own personal families. Our station family will help with critical incident stress management for members who have been working a scene that is a crisis, someone burned very badly, or a motorcycle accident victim that was decapitated, etc.

Our work family cluster helps us deal with those emotions and to get us back to our personal families. Stay strong for each other and help each other always. We do not want to see any more firefighter suicides.

#42. Profanity at the Fire Station

I have to say, that when I started my career in 1975 the language around the fire house was obnoxious to say the least. Every other word seemed to be a cuss word. Profanity in conversation seemed to go hand and hand with our job. Well, I am happy to say that over the last 30 years there has been a great adjustment for the better! There is much less profanity. I believe it is a shift in the family dynamics, respect given is respect earned, and more of our folks continuing their education levels. All of these initiatives help to achieve that goal to lower the usage of profanity around the home and fire station.

Profanity leaves a dirty mark I believe on those saying it and those having to hear it. I myself pay close attention to what words are coming out of my mouth so I do not offend others. When I hear a firefighter saying the words F— this or F— that, or using the M—F- - word, I cringe and then have to say something like "We really don't need that language." We have to watch what we say and how we say it!

#43. Obscene gestures on and off duty

I know of a case in metro Atlanta where a firefighter while driving his engine company through town was 'accidently cut off' by a driver switching lanes, and the firefighters/FAO response immediately was to show the car driver how he felt about that, and signaled to him with the 'middle finger' sign, as we know it from the famous 'Top Gun' movie where Goose and Maverick go inverted on top of a Mig 28 Russian fighter and Mav communicates with the pilot by giving him 'the finger' which prompts the Mig to bug out.

Well needless to say, the engine operator had to apologize and was reprimanded as a result of the complaint filed by the citizen/driver. Whether you are driving your engine company, or your personal pickup truck, act smart, no gestures.

#44. Ethical behaviors when out purchasing items

Always use good ethical business behavior when you are out purchasing anything. Never, ever take anything for free. Wearing your uniform and driving up in your engine company is not a free ride to all you need. In the supermarket you must pay the same prices as the customers in line with you. Some business owners and managers will want to give you a discount because you are a firefighter.

Free and discounted items sound like nice gestures however; it is unethical for us to accept. Other citizens that see or hear that, may not say anything right then, but will surely talk about how they felt it was wrong for us to get it half price or even free, and they had to pay full price. The citizen may complain. When offered, just say "We really appreciate your offer, however our department policy doesn't allow for it." and go on with your detail. Smart move!

#45. Use of your position for favors

This topic is a killer. If you get in the habit of using your position to obtain favors from people, then you have now put yourself in that unethical, immoral category. I know chief officers that would always make sure they wore their work uniforms complete with all his gold, white shirt, dress hat, etc., when they went shopping for anything, but especially for items like a house, car, looking at private schools and colleges with their children, as well as for services like roofers, painters, electricians, plumbers, anyone that would provide a service to their house etc. this is a bad choice!

What starts out to sound like a great idea, even to your family members, can end up disastrous. I'd like to show an example as to how an innocent act can look bad:

Let's say an engine company has a car dealership in their territory and the company officer has it on his list of buildings to inspect because they are going through some renovations. He and his crew suit up and ride over to the dealership. It just so happens that the company officer is looking for a new truck and has been eyeing one in particular. He loves it but the price is too high for him right now. Don't get me wrong, I'm not saying that this happens all the time, but it does and has happened. To make a long story short, while the crew is conducting their inspection which includes scouting out how much new sprinkler system will be needed during these renovations, the officer is talking with the manager about that special truck he has been admiring, but he doesn't have all the money right now to do it. Well, the manager feels almost compelled to help out and agrees to reduce the price so he can come back with his family and purchase it for the price he can afford, now that the manager has reduced the price.

What I didn't mention (yet), was that the inspection indicated that a decision had to be made by the company officer to include additional equipment which would cost the management an extra $10,000 to complete and the company officer could wave it based on a few changes in the plan. Well, as it turns out, the company officer signed off on the waiver and saved the dealership that extra $10,000. This type of activity should 'never' take place. Even though the code was covered in the renovations, the manager felt as though he had to assist the company officer in buying that new truck for that special price. As a rule of thumb, never show up representing your department in uniform if you are purchasing personal items. This will keep everyone on the ethical page together. It's best not to give off any bad vibes when you are dealing with fire department business in the community.

#46. Is borrowing items from your Department stealing?

This topic is not just addressed for firefighters. It is a general 'bad habit' to take, or borrow anything from your fire station/department. From pencils, pens, paper, use of the copier machine for personal use, using tools, equipment, even a truck for your personal use will put you in the category of being unethical.

Many co-workers who see you doing these things may say something to you, others may not, but their image of you may be diminished because you are really stealing from the department. We all need to purchase our own items for our own personal use. The work items and equipment are for work jobs and use, not for home jobs. Make good choices. Purchase your own items and then you won't have to be looking over your shoulder wondering.

#47. Fire Department assigned take home vehicles

I know that you will agree with me that this topic of who gets to take home a department vehicle when they are off duty has caused much discussion, and even arguments within the department.

Some departments have strict rules where only the fire chief will be allowed to take home his department assigned vehicle. The chief of the department is for all intent and purposes the only one that will need to have access to all his gear, and radio equipment including computers in the event of a manmade or natural disaster/incident.

The 'on duty' suppression folks already have all their apparatus, vehicles and equipment with them at their station.

Fire Marshal, Fire Arson Investigator, Fire Prevention Officer, PIO, each of these positions is a 'non' first response vehicle that needs to arrive within the designated response time to an incident. Not to say that they won't be needed at the call, what is being said is, those who are assigned to these positions and vehicles can drive to their station to pick them up and respond to the incident from there.

Most departments will not include these people and their vehicles as part of their list of emergency vehicles needed to handle a 911 Emergency.

Having said all that, I say it from two positions, first from what I wrote above, and second, those who drive these vehicles are always responsible for everything that happens when they have them in their care.

We have all heard stories of incidents occurring during off duty hours where the assigned driver of these non-emergency response (take home) vehicles had to explain a situation occurring off duty and they were driving their department vehicle. Incidents such as accidents, driving under the influence, seen leaving a dance club, taken to the mall with the family to shop, going out to a restaurant, shopping at Home Depot or Lowe's for their home projects, etc. So that it doesn't appear that I am calling out everyone but the chief, we have also heard of incidents of conduct unbecoming of the chief of departments. Use sound judgment.

#48. Being out of your response territory

I know we all have situations that come up in our personal lives while we are on our 24-hour tour that may need our attention. We also may need to handle a detail, or check on something that one of your engine company members is concerned about, but, if you handle any of them, you will be out of your assigned response area.

I know of a dual company on the west coast that thought it would be OK to drive out of their response territory to play an hour or two of tennis because there was an awesome court there. And another incident where an engine company crew member needed to drop by Home Depot and get some plumbing supplies so he could make a quick fix at home, which was also out of their response territory.

These two cases seem OK on the surface until you have to answer to your chief, or a citizen, why it took you so much longer to get to their fire call or medical call. Because they were out of their designated 911 Emergency Response Territory, they were delayed in getting to their calls.

Take a look at my suggested Do's and Don'ts for these two examples:

1. The entire station compliment went out of their territory for 'physical fitness'. Two hours of tennis.
   - Do – No one is saying not to exercise, or even play tennis, however the company officer should have advised his supervisor and 911 that they were going to be out of normal response territory and to respond the closer unit if a call came in.
2. The engine company crew member that needed to go to Home Depot to pick up supplies could have been done when he got off duty in the morning.
   - Do Not – Under any circumstances just leave your assigned response territory unless you have received permission from a superior officer and notified the 911 dispatch center so they would know to dispatch closer units if there was a call for service until you came back in service.

Both company officers were reprimanded for not following department suppression operations policies. Think before we act.

#49. Conducting community outreach in your station neighborhoods

Having served in the northeast (Boston) and the southeast (metro Atlanta) there is one thing I know for sure, and that is, your fire station neighbors, sure love having you there. If yours are like many, they will drop off pies, cakes, casseroles, cupcakes, and all sorts of goodies just out of the blue. Now, that is what I call a good neighbor relationship. I will share one story that proved to be the start of a great neighborhood relationship. Before I took the fire chief's position in Union City, GA, I would ride by their stations and notice that on most occasions the station overhead doors would be closed with personnel and equipment inside, especially on the weekend. Well, after I got on the job I started to evaluate the neighborhood to see how we could better interact. Below are a couple of Dos and Don'ts when trying to address the neighborhood interface.

Don't keep all your stations closed up like no one is home. If you are a volunteer department and no one is supposed to be home, then that is fine. If you are a career, full time, manned department, that is very different.

Don't make off to your neighbors that you are only interested in them if they have an emergency, other than that, they should only see you then.

Do keep your station doors open and actually feel free to stand or even sit out front of your stations and wave to your neighbors like you would in your own home neighborhoods. Let's face it, citizens pay taxes and the tax base in your city pays for salaries and benefits as well as your operating equipment. If they see you being open and friendly, they will feel better about paying their taxes and may even give an extra donation to your department.

Do one thing to get to know your neighbors. We sponsored a cookout at one of our multi family structure neighborhoods, with no pool, on one of those 95 to 100 degree days. We then laid up the 100-foot aerial and played off the 750GPM monitor hovering over the basketball court for a couple hours. Those kids and parents and the media loved us for that! Be creative and win!!

#50. Interfacing with your operational counterparts

This is one topic that I know you all have a lot to say about. It's never an easy task to get all public safety groups to agree and operate together and play nice all the time. This could mean off duty, and on duty, working incidents, and in the conference room planning budgets. The other departments could be public works, electrical, streets, code enforcement etc. Everyone wants to be in charge.

Does this sound familiar to you? It does to me. I was very happy when our police department started to adjust and adapt to our NIMS concepts. They saw how every chief could play their role and all play well together and accomplish the goals together. We even got it going so that the city manager, purchasing and finance, legal and other departments and sections found in the NIMS criteria were all playing their part. Below are a couple of Dos and Don'ts to consider.

Don't start a war with your police department especially if they also control the 911 communications center.

Don't try to play the city manager against any one department in an effort to look good in front of her or him.

Do be friendly towards all departments that operate within your organization's structure.

Do play nice when at meetings with other department members. Meaning; get along, don't be rude, and stay professional.

Do share all the information you may have on an upcoming event or potential incident. Trust is everything when it comes to public safety so act accordingly. Like your personnel's lives depend on it.

Do act mature and responsible in everything you do. It will pay off in the short and long run.

Do be kind!!!

CONCLUSION SUMMARY

Every once and a while, we all have to 'stop' and examine how we conduct ourselves in everything we do and every way we do it, in and out of the public and family eyes, on the job and off. This 'stopping' has happened to me every once and a while so I have a chance to re-evaluate how I am conducting my moral and professional business.

Sometimes I didn't like what I saw in myself and had to make changes. After my public sector fire service retirement, I see that life will continue to throw us those curve balls and provide temptations that will have you making choices. You can make the right ones or the wrong ones. I made a few of each.

By God's grace, I was able to finish a fire service career with some 30 years of personal and professional experiences that led me to write these top '50' Dos and Don'ts. Dos and Don'ts I consider important enough to share with you, some that would appear to be common sense ones, others more complex and of a delicate nature, but all the same, I have seen firefighters lose sight of their goals and make some minor errors in choice making up to and including those that will terminate your career. One of my former bosses would say, "Hey, that is a Career Limiting Move" or "Hey, that is a Career Ending Choice". It can be as minor as a chief using his work car to run errands, or as devastating as a chief showing up intoxicated on the fire scene and start giving orders that are not sound. These things have happened, and hopefully will not continue.

As 21st Century Firefighters, we need to be doing our job smarter and with a high moral aptitude. Every day we learn of another firefighter, lieutenant, captain, or chief officer being reprimanded, and even terminated for conduct unbecoming. I am reminded daily what can happen to you if you choose wrong. When we know the difference between right and wrong, know the consequences, and outcomes if we choose the wrong way, we will have to serve out our punishment. This could include a few days without pay, demotion, termination of position, and even a prison sentence.

I ask you to conduct a mental / moral check when you are reviewing these top '50' topics and see how you fare out. Be honest when doing it, even write them down and ponder over all of it. Only you will know the true answers to the questions. If you are not happy with what you see in writing, or how you feel, then this is the time to make changes in your life. If you don't change your behaviors that could be considered destructive, then the cycle will continue, and your daily situation will grow worse. You can make a difference in your life right now. Take the time to seek assistance from someone you trust that will help support and guide you to a happier better you!

Remember: **'You' Can Make The Difference**

"Work Safe-Work Smart-Go Home"

Chief T

ABOUT THE AUTHOR

 **Stan Tarnowski,** Fire Chief (ret), began his career in 1975 with the Boston Logan International Airport Fire Department serving in multiple operational and administrative positions. In metro Atlanta Georgia, he served as Fire Chief, 911 & EMA Director for the City of Union City. Deputy and Suppression Section Chief at the Georgia State Fire Academy, and Chief of Training for the Henry County Georgia Fire Department. Tarnowski received his associates degree in Fire Science (fire protection & safety technology) in 1976 from Bunker Hill Community College; holds several public safety certifications, is CFO designated, and is a Public Safety Training Instructor IV, and NPQ Board Certified Level IV Fire Instructor. He is currently the President of Firesafe Consulting Group.

Please visit my website at:

www.5AlarmMedia.com

You may also contact me directly via email:

ChiefT@5AlarmMedia.com

Also by this author

Putting a "Lid" on Food-On-The-Stove-Fires

PUTTING A "LID" ON
FOOD-ON-THE-STOVE
FIRES

Using 21st Century Technology
to Eliminate These Fires in
Your Community and
Save Lives and Property

FIRE CHIEF (RET.) STAN TARNOWSKI
WITH
BATTALION CHIEF (RET.) ROBERT AVSEC

Putting a "Lid" on Food-On-The-Stove-Fires was written to be a simple guideline for any and all fire departments wishing to make a direct impact on the reduction of stove top-pan fires which will ultimately reduce civilian and firefighter injuries, fatalities, and the loss of property throughout the country. The guideline is based on the recognition and use of available high end heat limiting technology (HEHLT) that can be installed on all electric coil type burners used for cooking. The premise is that the heat limiting sensor technology used in a conventional electric coil burner can stop the maximum heat at below the auto-ignition temperatures for normal cooking oils, hence eliminating the chance for pan fires to occur.

The guideline provides for a step by step process that is simple to use, and that every fire prevention office can put together for senior management (e.g. Fire Chief).

www.ingramcontent.com/pod-product-compliance
Lightning Source LLC
Chambersburg PA
CBHW070327290526
45791CB00003B/1282